THISTLE

Poems of Life

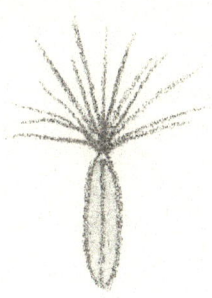

Elizabeth Anne Hin

Copyright © 2018 Elizabeth Anne Hin
All Rights Reserved

Illustrations Copyright © 2018 by Cynthia L. Kirkwood

Editing, Design, & Composition by Sarla V. J. Matsumura

Library of Congress Control Number: 2018946508

ISBN-13: 978-0692106440
ISBN-10: 0692106448

Printed in the United States of America

Published by Issa Press
Austin, Texas

DEDICATION

To My Spiritual Family

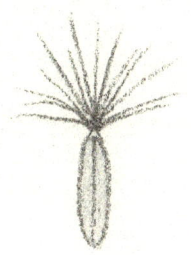

CONTENTS

No Matter What	1
There Were Swans	3
All is Well	5
There Was Lace	7
Brother	13
Three	15
On This Grey Day	17
Cygnets	21
Bouchée	23
Banjo	25
Queensland Blue	27
Limping	29
Three Roses	33
This Day	35
Casa Finca Vigia	37
Home~Wild Rose Ranch	39
Seventy	43
Nestlings	45
Birdhouse	47
Theron's Flowers	49
When the Water Came	51
Blessed Here	53
Patriarch	55
Wisteria	63
Blessed	67

NO MATTER WHAT

No matter
What
He prays
Head bowed
Or book turned
Arabic
Latin
Prayers of friends
Of every tongue
He remains attenuated to
Their conversations
With God
That is all
Really
He is
Ever
Paying attention
Towards
The threshold of Grace.
Holiness
Without
Any harm
God's son.

For Kabir Edmund Helminski

THERE WERE SWANS

There were swans
They had so many things to say
Calls
Cries
Words
Of
Sky
Sea
Cygnet
And
Abiding love
There is peace
Harmony
One path
For all
Swans

I opened the door
For them
To them
Please
Come in
Or
Wait
Oh

I shall
Come out

To the sea
Sky
Cygnets
I shall
Come out
I am with you

ALL IS WELL

There is a dove at our birdbath
A woman at our well
A man knelt in prayer here

And all is well

Our dove coos
Dun~colored
White tips fly
White~tipped feathers
Above our home into the sky

Into the wellspring
The woman's cup dips deep
That Heaven and life
To this man
Bring love, sweet love
And
Only love to keep

Rain fills the birdbath
The cup and the heart
With grace, always grace
Blessed grace
Thus we start

To pray

And
For this, for all, we give thanks, and
  thanks
And only thanks, ever thanks.

THERE WAS LACE

I.
Needles
Threaded
With
Silk
Into
Roses
Lilies
And
Swans

Lace
Bobbined
Through
Fingers
Moving
As Grandmothers
Aunties
And
Wise
Women
Had
Trained
Our
Hands
Toward
God

In
Floss
Of
Linen
For cloths
Handkerchiefs

Pieces
Of
Lace
For
All
The
Blessings
All
The
Occasions
Of
Precious
Life

Some
Of
The women
Fell
Lace
Torn
Between
Their souls
And those
Of acquaintances
Neighbors
Even of Mothers
And
Other
Relatives

She's
An enemy
She's
A conspirator

And
She
Oh,
Take
Her
She
Just
A woman
Whose
Lace
And
Silver
I will have
When
You
Take
Her

To the
Gas chamber
Or
The
Gun
Shot

You will
Take her
For
Me
Won't
You?
You know
How much

I want her lace

II.
Grandmother Anna
Your lace
Alsatian knots
Spun through
Your
Two
Hands
Soft
And strong
Upon
Your
Lap
Beside Mother
Father
Michael
And me
Complex
Harmonious
And infinitely
Beautiful
Your
Face to me
I remember
Your precious hands
Bobbined
Sitting
You
Heaven's
Living promise
Hair
Braided
And
Coiled
Atop
Your head

God etched
This
In
My soul
As you
Spun
For our
Paths
Ever
Safe
In
Your
One
Son's
One
Child's
Home
Daughter~in~law
Whom
You
Loved
Respected
Trusted
And
Raised
After
Their
Marriage
She
Would
Always
Be
Your
Daughter
Truly
Beloved

Finishing
A cloth
Lace
For her
For him
For me
For us
You had fingered
Many years
That
All the tables
Of my so loved
Life
Would be adorned
With your blessing,
Honor
Wisdom
And grace
I am a blessed woman
Grandma
Your lace
One thread
Of God
Unbroken
As
Your
Granddaughter

BROTHER

Brother
Of
Gentleness
And grace
Is your
Name
Wind
Water
Sea
Or
Sky
You
Who
Never
Hurt
Harm
Injure
Any
One
Or
Animal
Plant
Who held
Our
Great
Uncle Michael's
Hand
When
You
Were
So
Wee
Held
It fast
In

Your
Tiny hand
Of
Trust
And grace
Walking
With him
His
Tall
Lean
Frame
As yours
Is now
As he
Taught
You
Of tree
And
Dale
He whom Frank Lloyd trusted
With waterfalls and cliffs
Only with Uncle Michael
Was Wright willing to build
Fallingwater

Only with you coming
To Earth
Later
Younger brother
Of goodness
And grace
Was I willing
To be born.

For Peter William Hin

THREE

Three Blue Jays
Fourth, a mate
Close at wing
In a tree
One Cardinal
Spouse nearby
In a flowering
Tall bower
And a Dove
At the birdbath
For conversation
And water
One race
Avian
Many colors
The Great Peace.

ON THIS GREY DAY

On this grey
Soft
Day
At the Sea

There are lichens
At my feet
Mosses
In flower
Midsummer light
Trees fulfilled
In
Leafed splendor

European Ravens
Of
Grey and black
Magpies
Of grey and black
And white
Ocean birds
To whom
I have not
Yet
Been
Formally
Introduced
And
Sparrows
Grey and black
Tawny shades
And perfect

And
Small darling birds
Of unknown names
And
Birds
Of
Songs
Of the
North
Of
White nights
Nests high in branches
Human nests beneath
Of brick
And wood

Shall we live
Then
As
Vulnerable
As
Real
Vast
Humble
Modest
And
True

As
Are
All
Beings

Even
We
Human
Birds
Human
Trees
Human
Men
Human
Women

On this grey
Day
This soft
Soft
Day

CYGNETS

You
Who
Are

Created
All

Ever

And
Beauty

Clouds
Swans upon the Northern seas

Carrying
When needed
As needed

Cygnets

Their babies
Baby swans

Cygnets

Upon
Their
Backs

Showing
Them
Cygnets
This way

Home

BOUCHÉE

Bouchée
Beautiful cat
You await me
With love unfailing
And
The most shy
Certain persona
Nature sweet and good
Steadfast and
Not strong
But real
As are we all
When
As innocent
And true
As are
You
Our beautiful cat
Eleven years now

BANJO

You are our
Darling
Darling kitten
Almost six
Kitten ever
Kitten always
Clear as starlight
Faithful
As
The
Best dog
Curious
Brilliant
In consciousness
Beside us
Lucky
Banjo
We are blessed.

QUEENSLAND BLUE

Tobe
Naughty
Dog
Shepherding
Us
Every breath
Every moment
Sense
Snort
Howl
And Scratch
Nuance
Of
Who
And
What
You
Are
Working
Boy
Go
Get
Your
Dad
Life
Is
Your
Joy
Serious
And
Perfect

LIMPING

Her
Leg
Is broken
Like
Mine

She walks
Without suffering
As I do

Lives
Scarred
Yet
So
Content

She comes
For the corn
My Darling
Places

Feeds to her
Her Sister
Other deer
Black squirrels
Cardinals
Doves
And

Her serene eyes
Wide set
In that darkened
Heart~shaped face
We have so, so loved

Come to know well
These years

Her life
Is
As perfect
As mine

Coyotes stalking her
New urbanites
Wishing the deer
Of Austin
Would go away

Now that they
The urbanites
Have arrived
Here
From
Somewhere

But
My deer
Makes me happy
Every time I see her
It is perfect

Her
God
The Universe
Her recognition of us
Undisturbed and
Knowing

Her face and mine
As we regard one another
So deeply
So truly

Her place
Here
In this Cosmos
As holy
And as real
As anything
Any of us
Shall ever know
Or do
Or be

A perfect deer
Limping up
The steep hill
Of the deer trail

Of many years
Of many deer
Of many generations

Here
At our home
At her home

THREE ROSES

Three roses
Up
Over the wall
Above the Jasmine
Toward the sun
And moon
The light
In the soft
Breeze
Of this
Morning

Just
As
Three children
Now
Adults
Young
Toward the sun
And moon
And in
The great
Human heart
Blossom

Such grace.

THIS DAY

A
Candle
This
Day

Her
Day
Of
Tears
And
Roses
This
Day

Champagne
Prosecco
Such
Love
Of
God
Family

And
Seeking
All
That
Is
Real

This
Day

And
Every
Day
I
Have
Known
Her

Candlelight
This
Day

For Sarla V. J. Matsumura

CASA FINCA VIGIA

Beneath the palms
Royal
Verdant
At the house
Of the writer
I have loved
In words and characters
Of life
Since I was
A girl
I am blessed
By his gift
Of words
Seeking
Love
And wish for peace
He had such sorrow
And illness
That
He could not bear
That which
He was seeking
'Ava Gardner was the most beautiful white
   animal on the planet'
A guide walking by quotes Hemingway
But the birds
Rooster
Call
And
Breeze sing
Softly
Through the trees
Bamboo

Here
With
My Darling
And Fabio
Safely
Shepherding us
Cuba
Troubled
Yet so precious
This beloved nation
This beloved people

HOME~WILD ROSE RANCH

Turned
To the East
On this
Soft day
Pale grey
Clouds
Face
Toward
The breeze
On his land
Noble
Countenance
His two
Elder
Of three
Daughters
And
Son
Are
Going
To cut
Mesquite
Learn
At his side
Today
Just as
The posture
Of
His Father
Who
Would
Stand
Ride
Work
Drive his truck

Visit
But
Mostly
Be
A great soul

Turned
To the East
South
West
And North
Checking the water
Placing the feed
Trailering to auction
Several head
Toward a fair price
Prayed
Hoped
Worked for
From the old boys
Who were
Big and small
In stature
Of ethic
And life
Because
By God
He was
Worthy
Of
Truth
And so
This son
My Darling
And that
Son's
Daughter

Son
And little one
Third child
A daughter
Are Fathered
Our three
Children

Turned
Heavenward
At every breath
To be
As beautiful
As rare
And
Real
As the
Wild Roses
Today
At the
Gate
Of the
Beloved ranch.

SEVENTY

Her hair
Is
Silver
Now
And
Beautiful
As
Is
She
Eyes
Steady
Blue
As
A
Sapphire
Dedicated
To
Truth
This soul
Her heart
Full
Of freedom
Of care
Love
Dedication
Poppies
And
So very
Many flowers

Blooming
Just as
Does she
In God
And
Everywhere,
Seventy.

NESTLINGS

Nestlings
Wrens
And
Doves
Call
To us
Babes
At
The birdhouse
Attended
By parents
As dutiful
As you
As true
Cheeping
Ensemble
Just as
Your children
Now adult
Call
Not yet,
Dad,
Please.

BIRDHOUSE

That
Most
Tender
Home
Of
Our
Home
Is
Silent
Today
At
The
Birdhouse

All of
The
So
Precious
Wrens
Have
Flown
Father
And
Mother
Now
To
Teach
Beloved
Fledglings

In the
Sky
And
All
Around
Us
Seeking
Food
Shelter
Safely
Silent
At the
Nest.

THERON'S FLOWERS

Theron's flowers
Nanda's blossoms
Blessed
Are in the garden
They are here, too
Poppy petals fluttering
Iris in fleur de lis prayer
As symbol
And truth
Living
Fragrant
In holy color
Petals as fragile
As the Poppies
As Nanda
Theron
Lady
Lavender queen.

For Theron Nanda Tuttle

WHEN THE WATER CAME

And when the water came
Those hundreds
Those thousands
Miles away
I said why
Deluge
Grief of Grandmother

Field
And calf
Watersodden buildings
In muck
Stinking of mold
Sewage
And such

While islands to the East
Blown dry
By winds and waters
Deforested
Deleafed
Villages flattened
Birds without shade
Seeking
Branches with foliage
And finding none

BLESSED HERE

Beyond the deer
Black~eared
Tall conifers
Behind her
Ahead of her
Now
As she turns
Away
On ribbon road
Softest snow
Falling
All about
Our son driving us
Lodge
Above
Cratered lake
Of clearest waters
Hidden
In midst
Whitened sky
Iced flakes
Then
Long
After dawn
Snow as powder
In almost silence
But still
Heard
Falling
To roof
And gable top
At our windows
We dreamt
Our sleep
Our stay

Our beautiful meal
A dinner
Of Patriarchs
One
Would have been
A century old this year
One resting in God and
Body to rest gently
Within this Earth
And one to turn
To sixty~fifth year
And son at the helm
Threshold of the
Deep
Good
Man
Great
I hope

This morn
We rise
Out into the white
First Winter
High
In the South
Of the Cascades
Toward the Sea
We will drive
Blessed here
In the mountains
A white out

PATRIARCH

He is
Known
In the
Very
Heart
Of this
Land
Water
Sky
And
Sun above

Remembered
In every
Curve
Of this
Loved
Long
Verdant
Portion
Of
The river

Wonderful
Casting
His dreams
Toward
The sea
Every year
Pretty much
These many
Years

Dreams
Of life
Sometimes
Of
The great
Fish
All Salmon Family
Chinook
Silver
Dolly Varden
Rainbow
Steelhead
Each
In its
Season

His pole
Is
Tended
The hook
Weight
Line
Net
Gear
Such fun
The best
Smiles
Deepest heart
Almost
Of every year
Fine days
Of fun
And meaning

Temperate
Cool
But
Not too
Rainy
And
Not too
Yet
Fresh
Trees turning
Season
Toward
Winter
Splendid joy
The Salmon
Are running
Not feeding
Feeding
Sometimes

He is
Quite old
Not too old
A good old
Like
The Salmon
This Autumn
And
Every Autumn

Swimming
Upriver
In all
His glory
Nose hooked
To protect
His path

His Family's
Skin turned
Copper and green
His spawn
Now set
To flourish
Throughout
The mountains
Valleys
And
Dales
Of the West
Of the
Whole World
Everywhere

Where shall
I
And
What work
And
When shall
I marry
Have a baby
Choose a
Home
Grandpa
His progeny
Plaintively ask
Exploring river
Stream
Lake
Cove
Harbor

Of life
In all
Their
Young
Stages

When
It is
Time,
He answers
Son
Daughter
Grandson
Granddaughter

Time
To harvest
Nuts,
Fruit
Time
To water
Time
To plant
Time
To rest
Time
To cook
Time
To
The cabin
For humor
For love

True intimacy
Faith
And trust
Toward
Wisdom
Modesty
And
Balance

When
It is
Time
When
It is
Time

And he
Contemplates
When he
Walked
The shore
Casting
That rod
When
A boy
Once
Upon
A time
Harvesting
Some
Steelhead
Rainbow Trout

Or such

Another time
When
A young man
With
That net
Of
His Father's
When
It was
Time

And
Every time
Husband
Father
Farmer
Rancher
Every time
Sentiment of
Such
Goodness
In this man
Every year
Every chapter

Of his life

Each time
He turned
Casting
Into the
Very grace
Of
The stream
The river
Toward
The sea

Honest
And true
Always
Old man
Patriarch
Oceanic
Fisherman

For Jacare Cordoza's Grandpa
and his Family

WISTERIA

A
Bower
At
Her
School

Over
A
Veranda

A
Walking
Pathway
Bedecked
With
Petals

To class
To Home
To Meal
To Office

As
She
Awakens
Matures
Into
The
Woman

She is
To
Become

Root
Into
Stem
Into
Trunk
Into
Vine
Into
Branch
Into
Bud
Into
Blossom
And
Bower

Human being
Into
Daughter
Into
Sister
Into
Beloved
Into
Colleague
Into
Mentor
Into
Friend

And
Perhaps
Mother
Someday

This
Day
Into
Wise
And
Tender
Woman

She blooms
With
All
The beauty

And
Grace
Of
Wisteria.

For Mackenzie Meredith Gabriel

BLESSED

We met
A couple
With
The very
Sweetest
Faces

Fresh
As the dew
Of the mornings
Days
Or nights
On which
They were
Each
Conceived
And
Born

Faces
Marked
Not
By loss
But
By transformation
Into the gratitude
Of being
A human

Etched in kindness
And
Experience
Simply
Of
Life

Wise
Noble
Tender
Humble
And free
To love
Know
Contemplate

And
Walking
With
Cane
Arm
In
Arm
Entwined

So
Very
Slowly
Down
The
Hotel
Stairway
Through
The Garden
Pathway

To
The
Shore
Of
Lake
Windermere

A promenade
For me
Of all
That a
Human
Might
Hope
To
Become

Never
Will
Two finer
People exist
Than they

Blessed.

ABOUT THE AUTHOR

Elizabeth Anne Hin studied poetry formally with George E. Dimock, Richard Wilbur, William Hoover Van Voris, Michael Benedikt, Elizabeth Hardwick, Sir Stephen Spender, and Joseph Brodsky. Her Mother read poetry aloud from *A Child's Garden of Verses* by Robert Louis Stevenson and from other cherished texts from Beth's conception through childhood. Her Father taught her through his admiration for Homer's life, work, and virtuous message, from the world's classics and histories, and from noble and heroic peoples and cultures of all nations. He practiced his faith in the equality of all men and women, and in all aspiration: 'Ad astra per aspera,' ~Seneca. Her Mother was a private living example of this virtue.

Beth has embraced poetry, from reading to writing, since youth, observing in gratitude the poetry infused in sculpture at Wellington's port in New Zealand and attending readings by Jorge Luis Borges at the 92nd Street YMCA in Manhattan, New York, Adrienne Rich in a hallowed hall of Amherst, Massachusetts, Drummond Hadley and Gary Snyder in Anchorage, Alaska, Mary Oliver at a Presbyterian Church in Dallas, Texas. She has been shown kindness in mentoring by writers from John Updike to Carlos Fuentes, Richard Erdoes to Derek Walcott; and by W. S. Merwin, who expressed to her in 1973 that he had written nearly every day since the age of 21, and requested of Beth that she do the same.

ALSO BY ELIZABETH ANNE HIN

The Grail: A Story of Issa and Yeshua, 2014
Jdg: Poems of Love, 2016
Live Oak: Poems of Texas, 2016
Willow: Poems of Devotion, 2016
Birch: Poems of Love, 2018
Sequoia: Poems of Eternity, 2018

Published by Issa Press, Austin Texas

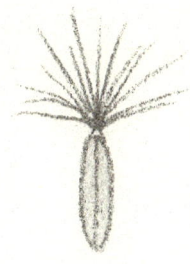

www.ingramcontent.com/pod-product-compliance
Lightning Source LLC
Chambersburg PA
CBHW022119090426
42743CB00008B/922